TC 3/7

TABLE OF CONTENTS

INTRODUCTION

Politicians talk about a grand bargain in America. If you work hard, you can have a comfortable middle class job or better. Any career is possible regardless of one's ethnicity or socio-economic status at birth.

Unfortunately, the reality in America today is not even close to this ideal. A staggering disparity exists between college completion rates for students from wealthy and low-income families in the United States. According to a 2015 article in the Wall Street Journal, nationally only 9% of students from lowest quartile income families earn a college degree by the time they turn twenty-four. However, 77% of students from highest quartile income families earn a college degree by the time they turn twenty-four[1].

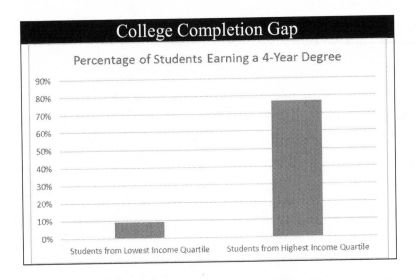

In the 21st century a college education is critical. A report from the McCourt School of Public Policy at Georgetown forecasts that by 2018, 63% of all jobs will require at least some postsecondary education. The vast majority of jobs that pay enough to allow a middle-class lifestyle or better require a college degree. As the chart below illustrates, individuals with a college degree earn significantly more than those with a high school degree or less.

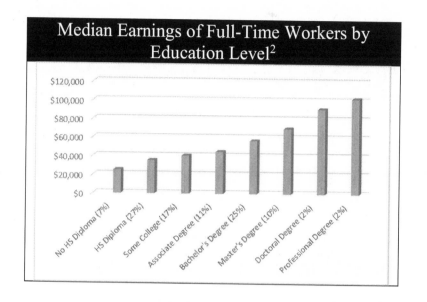

Median Earnings of Full-Time Workers by Education Level[2]

The traditional public school systems in most of America's urban cores have failed students for decades. Millions of students from low-income families have not had access to high-quality K-12 education. The result for many is a lack of available opportunities. There is no mystery as to why our inner cities are plagued by high unemployment, crime, and violence. If people are not educated, they do not have good opportunities. If they do not have good opportunities, they are much more likely to get involved in criminal activities and end up in the criminal justice system.

Education is a huge and important civil rights issue. To have a fair shot at the American Dream, all children must have the opportunity to have the preparation and skills to succeed in college. African-Americans are much more likely to live in a zip code that has failing public schools and thus have been disproportionately impacted by the failure of our nation's urban public school systems. The state of K-12 education in America's inner cities is not only a tremendous social injustice, but is in direct conflict with the American Dream ethos inspired by the Constitution.

One's destiny in America should not be largely determined by one's zip code and it does not need to be. In Kansas City where I grew up, the traditional public school district has been failing children for decades. Fortunately, in 1998, Missouri passed a charter school law which allowed others to operate public schools within the boundaries of the Kansas City Missouri School District ("KCMSD"). Charter public schools have collectively transformed the educational opportunities available for thousands of students in the KCMSD.

In 2016 charter public schools educated roughly 40% of the K-12 public school students living within the boundaries of the KCMSD. This level of market share is in the top five in the nation behind New Orleans, Detroit, and Washington, DC. Charter public schools have created a competitive educational landscape which has created an incentive for the traditional school district to improve. While the traditional Kansas City Missouri School District is still far from high-quality, it has shown meaningful improvement in recent years actually achieving its highest rating from the state in three decades for the 2015-2016 school year.

Charter public schools were created in the early 1990's to improve our nation's public school systems. Charter schools are public schools and like traditional public schools, are funded by local, state and federal tax dollars based on student enrollment. They are free and do not have special entrance requirements. Charter schools are not religious and cannot discriminate against students on any basis. Just like traditional public schools, charter public schools are accountable for state and federal academic standards. As of 2016, there were more than 6,700 charter schools operating in 42 states and the District of Columbia educating nearly 3 million children[3].

Today, K-12 education within the boundaries of the Kansas City Missouri School District is at an inflection point. There is even optimism among local education reform practitioners that a significant majority of the students in Kansas City, Missouri could be getting a high-quality education within a decade. Hopefully, this book will shed light on the progress that has taken place and potentially serve as a roadmap for others who have the desire and will to address failing inner-city school systems.

For the last decade as Chairman of University Academy (UA), a K-12 college-preparatory charter public school that serves 1000 students who reside in the boundaries of the KCMSD, I have seen that it is possible for low-income students to achieve at the highest levels. I have also witnessed how multiple charter public schools can collectively create a competitive educational landscape that benefits students and the community.

University Academy opened its doors in 2000 and is one of the largest charter public schools in Kansas City. By Missouri law, all students who attend charter public schools must live in the district and be selected by lottery. Over 95% of the student body at University Academy is African-American and roughly 75% qualify for free or reduced lunch.

The mission of University Academy is to prepare students to succeed in an institution of higher education and to become leaders in society. 53% of the school's alumni who have been out of high school for 6 years or longer have completed a 4-year bachelor's degree. This is more than 5x the national average for students from lowest quartile income families (9%).

In August 2015, Newsweek Magazine published their "America's top high schools" issue and ranked University Academy the 199th best high school in the country in the "beating the odds" category. Additionally, for the fifth year in a row, University Academy's High School was recognized for excellence by U.S. News & World Report.

For the 2015-2016 academic year, University Academy received 100% on its Annual Performance Report from the State of Missouri which equates to Accredited with Distinction (versus 70% for the KCMSD). University Academy's High School ranked #1 out of 397 public high schools based on state of Missouri test scores for the 2015-2016 academic year[4].

Additionally, in 2016, University Academy's High School was one of fifty-four schools in the country to be named a National Title I Distinguished School. This honor, given by the National Title I Association, recognizes exceptional student performance.

In 2017 University Academy was nominated for National Blue Ribbon Schools recognition. This award, given by the U.S. Department of Education, is considered the highest honor an American K-12 school can receive. Less than ½ of 1% of schools in the nation are nominated for the award in any given year.

How is University Academy getting vastly different results with the same students? I believe our success has largely been driven by:

- A very clear mission and vision
- A culture of high expectations and accountability
- An incredibly dedicated and talented faculty and staff
- A rigorous college preparatory academic program

- Supplemental high value educational opportunities for K-12 students including a very robust summer study abroad program for high school students (71% of our class of 2017 will have participated in study abroad while in high school).
- Working with Alumni after they graduate through an Alumni Success Program

Charter public schools are governed by boards of directors. In this book, I explore the role the board plays in creating a high performing school as well as discuss some of the innovative programs we have created to support UA's mission. The practices discussed in this book can easily be copied and by replicating programs and practices that are working, we can improve education in America. My hope is that the information in this book will be helpful to other schools, nonprofits, practitioners, educators, and policy makers.

AUTHOR'S NOTE

I grew up in Kansas City, Missouri. From kindergarten through 12th grade I attended the Pembroke-Hill School, a private school. My parents never discussed sending my brother or me to public school. Given how terrible the Kansas City Missouri School District was in the late 1980s, I was extremely fortunate that my parents could afford to send me to an excellent school. The majority of the children my age in Kansas City, MO were not as lucky.

My parents were very supportive in all regards, but especially when it came to education. Going to college was always part of the plan. My parents regularly told my brother and me that they would pay for college and graduate school if we wanted to pursue that as well. Additionally, they were supportive of experiential learning opportunities like sleepaway camp and study abroad.

After second grade my parents started sending me to camp every summer. I went to Camp Nebagamon in Lake Nebagamon, WI for 5 years. Then I spent one summer at Sanborn Western Camps in Florrisant, CO. These summer camp experiences were not only fun, but were among my first experiences living independently from my family.

Sometime during 10th grade, my parents introduced me to Bob Schweich, a friend of my father's from when he went to Camp Nebagamon. Bob would end up having a huge impact on my life. Bob was a securities analyst on Wall Street, but also a huge advocate of study abroad for high school students. As a high school student, Bob had participated in summer abroad programs in the Netherlands and Denmark with the Experiment in International Living. As a result of Bob's encouragement, I went on an Experiment in International Living France Homestay/Travel program after my junior year in high school. This 6-week program ignited a lifelong curiosity and interest in other countries and cultures.

I attended college at The University of Michigan. The second semester of my sophomore year I went abroad again, this time on a semester in Kenya with the National Outdoor Leadership School. When I returned for my junior year, I focused my studies on economic and political development in Africa. I created my own major (Development Strategies for Africa) by getting sponsors in the economics and political science departments. In the spring semester of my junior year I went on Semester at Sea and learned about and visited Venezuela, Brazil, South Africa, Kenya, India, Malaysia, Hong Kong. Taiwan, and Japan. The highlight was Bishop Desmond Tutu being on the ship from Brazil to South Africa. When we arrived in Cape Town he hosted a reception at his official residence, Bishopscourt.

After college, I served for two years in the Peace Corps in Mali, West Africa. I lived near the Niger River in a mud house with no electricity or running water. My largest project was initiating and managing the establishment of a savings and credit bank in a community of 10,000 people with no previous banking institution. I also designed and supervised a 30-acre rice production project funded by the United States Agency for International Development. My formal assignment was working with the Malian Ministry of Health to transform a state run rural clinic into a self-funding health center.

The Peace Corps was one of the most amazing and important experiences of my life. I learned a lot of things from the Malian people. Despite terrible poverty, I saw widespread hospitality and generosity. I came to appreciate that people who live in extreme poverty are the same as people anywhere, especially when it comes to wanting the best for their children.

After the Peace Corps, I started law school at Stanford. I had applied to law and business schools at four different universities from Mali. I was accepted at both programs only at Michigan, but I wanted to have a new experience. Additionally, I couldn't pass up the opportunity to study at Stanford Law School. I figured I would re-apply to Stanford Business School during my first year of law school and certainly I would be accepted since I would be a member of the university community. However, it was not meant to be. Stanford Business School rejected me again, but fortunately I was accepted by Columbia Business School. I ended up working out a program that allowed me to do a bi-coastal JD and MBA in 4 years. I graduated with both degrees in May 2000.

Since graduate school, I have spent my business career in financial services; first as an investment banker at Lehman Brothers in New York City and since then in the investment business.

I recognize how fortunate I am to have grown up with such incredible educational opportunities. My own experience impacts my perspective greatly.

Chapter 1

The Search for a Big Project

In December of 1993 my father turned 60. To celebrate his birthday my parents planned a family cruise to Alaska. My brother and I asked to bring girlfriends, but my parents wanted to have a trip with just their two boys. They said "no" assuring us that there would be lots of young people on the boat.

Helzberg Diamonds, my family's retail jewelry business, was doing well. My parents had supported a variety of charitable causes, but they were now thinking about the possibility of taking on a big project – something that was not being addressed and could have an important impact in Kansas City. Instead of girlfriends, my parents asked my brother and me to bring philanthropic ideas that met their criteria to discuss on the birthday cruise.

It turned out that the average age of the people on the boat was about eighty. We ended up spending a lot of time on the trip discussing various community challenges and the potential for impact. We kept coming back to K-12 education in Kansas

City, MO as the most important area that needed help.

After the birthday trip, my parents, Shirley and Barnett Helzberg spent several years investigating various programs which could potentially improve K-12 education in Kansas City, Missouri. They explored voucher programs, after-school programs, and even the idea of setting up a private school. They talked to numerous people and learned about K-12 education wherever they could.

One of the first people my parents talked to was Peter Brown, their attorney. Peter and his wife Lynne, a former school teacher, were also interested in education. Together the four of them went to a conference sponsored by The Walton Family Foundation. The conference was primarily about the Children's Educational Opportunity Foundation of America (CEO America) school voucher program. CEO America was the umbrella for 36 voucher programs across the country providing up to half the private school tuition for 12,000 students from low-income families.

After the conference, my father reached out to Tom Bloch, the former CEO of H&R Block to get his thoughts on voucher programs. A few years earlier Tom had made national news when he left his job as CEO of H&R Block to become a teacher. At the time, Tom was teaching math at St. Francis Xavier, a parochial school serving inner-city students.

Tom was also thinking about how to create high-quality K-12 educational opportunities but wasn't interested in vouchers. Tom was just beginning to explore the idea of starting a charter school or even converting St. Francis Xavier to a charter school, an idea the Diocese of KC-St. Joseph later rejected. My father and Tom ended up spending most of the meeting talking about charter schools. Tom suggested that my father go hear one of the nation's foremost charter school experts, Dr. Joe Nathan, who happened to be coming to Kansas City to speak on the topic.

At some point in 1995 or 1996, my father went to Dr. Joe Nathan's speech about charter public schools. Joe was the founder and Executive Director of the Center for School Change. Joe had spent the early part of his career as an educator serving in a variety of teaching and administrative roles. However, at the time, his primary role was being an advocate and resource to promote strong charter school laws and strong charter public schools. Joe helped create the nation's first charter public school law in his home state of Minnesota in 1991 and went on to help create roughly 30 more state charter laws around the country.

My father was inspired by Joe's speech. He invited Joe to go to Arthur Bryant's BBQ to discuss starting a charter school. Over BBQ he asked Joe "Can you run it like a business?" meaning can you set goals, hire and fire people, and test new ways of doing things. Joe responded that you absolutely could. After the dinner my father was convinced that starting a charter public school could be a great way to impact K-12 education. Unfortunately, at that time, the State of Missouri did not have a charter school law.

Tom and my father had another meeting to talk about charter schools. My father asked Tom about the possibility of starting a school in Kansas where there was a charter law. Tom shared why he felt it made sense to wait for Missouri to pass charter legislation. The Kansas law was weak because charter schools could only be authorized by traditional public school boards. Tom was aware that there were ongoing efforts to get a strong law passed in Missouri and suggested "Waiting for Missouri to pass a charter law."

Chapter 2

The Kansas City Missouri School District

In 1954, the Supreme Court, decided the case of *Brown v. Board of Education*, which banned separate-but-equal schools. Ironically, an unintended consequence of this landmark civil rights case was the collapse of America's inner-city school systems.

The Kansas City Missouri School District ("KCMSD") is a case study on how the *Brown v. Board of Education* decision impacted urban school districts across the country. Paul Ciotti detailed the unravelling of the KCMSD in Cato Institute Policy Analysis No. 298 and much of the information below is from his work. I highly encourage anyone interested in a more comprehensive history of how the Kansas City Missouri School District unraveled to read his article. It is important to keep in mind that many of the things that happened in Kansas City played out in a similar fashion in inner-cities around the country.

In the mid-1950s the Kansas City Missouri School District served roughly 70,000 students.

The District was considered high-quality. At the time, roughly 75% of the students were Caucasian and 25% were minority. When I was growing up, many of Kansas City's most successful entrepreneurs, lawyers, doctors, and educators had graduated from KCMSD schools.

In the decades after *Brown v Board of Education*, wealthier families (primarily Caucasians) fled the district. Voters declined to approve any tax increases for the district after 1969. By the mid-1970s, the district had shrunk to roughly 36,000 students and roughly 75% of the students were African-American. As wealthier students left the district, the leadership of the district declined. The school board failed to effectively manage the quality of the district's operations and the school system continued to deteriorate[5].

In 1977, an attorney named Arthur Benson sued the state of Missouri on behalf of a number of Kansas City, MO school children. The suit alleged that the state had caused racial segregation within the district. The case was assigned to Judge Russell Clark, a newly appointed federal judge[6].

The trial didn't start until late 1983 and the case was not decided until 1987. Judge Clark found that the district and the state were "jointly and severally liable" for the segregated conditions in the KCMSD schools. This meant that if the district did not have the money, the state was responsible for the whole amount[7].

Judge Clark did not determine an amount for damages, instead he basically created an open checkbook for the district to spend the state's money. The idea was that the district would have the resources to make the school system so great that Caucasians would come back to the district schools and it would no longer be segregated[8].

The district was totally unequipped to spend money thoughtfully, strategically, or efficiently. Hundreds of millions of dollars were spent building new facilities and remodeling old ones. Waste and corruption were widespread. The District's central office bureaucracy became more and more bloated. The KCMSD was so top-heavy that a 1991 audit discovered that 54 percent of the district's budget never made it to the classroom; rather, it was used for food service, transportation, and, most of all, central administration[9].

The school board did not provide effective governance for the district. In 1997, the KCMSD had had 10 superintendents in the last nine years, most of them bought out or fired. With such turnover, it was hard to get anything accomplished that would have benefitted students. The turnover problem also left the district without the political will to do anything about improving the quality of teachers and principals[10].

Before the desegregation plan, the KCMSD had argued for more than 30 years that it did not have the money to offer high enough salaries to attract a first-class teaching staff. But even after the desegregation money started rolling in, the district still did not do anything to upgrade instructional personnel. It was easier and more politically palatable to spend money on expensive things like new buildings and new equipment. The District did not address things that really make a difference in education like appointing excellent principals, supervising instructional practices, developing curriculum, hiring good teachers, and firing bad ones[11].

In June 1995, with $1.6 billion having been spent by the KCMSD and no end in sight, the U.S. Supreme Court made its third ruling in the case, telling Clark to quit trying to solve social problems beyond his purview and, as soon as possible, return control to local authorities[12].

Two years later in March 1997, Judge Clark began the process of dismantling the desegregation plan by approving an agreement between the state of Missouri and the school district that would end the state's annual $110 million desegregation payment to the KCMSD after 1999[13].

In 1999, when the State made its final payment, the KCMSD had managed to spend a total of roughly $2 billion. Despite the incredible amount spent from 1987 through 1999, the district had continued to deteriorate. Academic achievement had declined and discipline and other problems had increased. By 1999, only about 28,000 students remained in the district. The vast majority of these students were from families that had little choice other than to stay in the district due to their economic situation[14].

The district's failure obviously had nothing to do with resources, it had to do with a lack of management. Adults' interests were placed ahead of children's interests. The KCMSD provided a consistent paycheck for many adults, but little value for the majority of its students.

The traditional Kansas City Missouri School District had a monopoly on K-12 public education in Kansas City. It had no incentive to be excellent and there was no accountability for results. Teachers and administrators that were not serving students were kept on the payroll. Collective bargaining agreements made it extremely hard for ineffective teachers and administrators to be fired. The district became a bloated bureaucracy that delivered very poor educational services to the community.

Interestingly, in 1967, Dr. Kenneth B. Clark, the psychologist who co-authored the "doll test" study which was used to help justify the *Brown v. Board of Education* decision, presented a paper at the National Conference on Equal Educational Opportunity in America's Cities. Dr. Clark's remarkable paper, subsequently published in the Harvard Educational Review, was titled "Alternative Public School Systems". Dr. Clark asserted that America's urban public school systems suffered from "pervasive and persistent" inefficiencies. He warned of the dangers of educational monopolies noting that "As long as local school systems can be assured of state aid and increasing federal aid without the accountability which inevitably comes with aggressive competition, it would be sentimental, wishful thinking to expect any significant increase in the efficiency of our public schools". He went on to say "Alternatives—realistic, aggressive, and viable competitors—to the present public school systems must be found. The development of such competitive public school systems will be attacked by the defenders of the present system as attempts to weaken the present system and thereby weaken, if not destroy, public education. This type of expected self-serving argument can be briefly and accurately disposed of by asserting and demonstrating that truly effective competition strengthens rather than weakens that which deserves to survive."[15] I highly recommend reading his paper as it turned out to be quite prescient.

Low-income children generally come into kindergarten already behind their higher income peers. Many have not been exposed to the volume and quality of words and many have not had access to early education. Despite this, hundreds of high-performing charter public schools around the country have demonstrated that low-income children can consistently achieve at the highest levels. However, this does not just happen. It takes a real commitment on the part of the students, families, and school.

The focus of a school system must be educating its students. Children's interests must be put ahead of adults' interests. One of the big advantages that charter schools have over traditional districts is that they are typically non-union. At charter public schools, teachers and administrators can be fired if it is in the best interest of the school. Decisions can be completely based on what is good for students.

Traditional public school Superintendents are hired to turn around failing school districts. Yet they do not have the ability to get rid of low-performing staff making real improvement almost impossible. If a company tried to recruit a new CEO to turn around a business, and told the CEO candidate that he/she could not fire low performers, he/she would not accept the job. Yet, this is the norm in K-12 traditional public school districts in America due to collective bargaining agreements negotiated by teachers' unions. While these agreements do protect an employee from being wrongfully terminated, they also prevent bad teachers who are not serving students well from being terminated. Protecting students from ineffective teachers is more important than protecting adults from being wrongfully terminated.

The failure of the Kansas City Missouri School District is typical of traditional public urban school districts around the country. This is a national problem.

Chapter 3

Charter School Legislation in Missouri

The story behind Missouri's charter school legislation began back in 1983 with a Republican Missouri lawmaker named Franc Flotron. Flotron was in the Missouri House of Representatives from 1982-1988 and the Missouri Senate from 1989-2000.

Flotron had been a school choice advocate for many years actually having introduced a voucher bill as far back as 1983. That bill was crushed in the Senate. Flotron unsuccessfully introduced stand-alone charter school bills in Missouri starting in 1991 and each year after. However, 1998 was different.

In 1998, the state was passing legislation to end the desegregation cases with Kansas City and St. Louis and finally some leverage existed to make it happen. The Charter school law was an amendment to the legislation to settle the desegregation cases. The bill was sponsored by Flotron and two democrats. It passed in the Senate and was given to the House. Unfortunately, in the House the charter school amendment was taken out in committee. However, a Democrat named Marsha

Campbell added it back on the House floor[16]. The bill passed and was signed into law by the Governor. Backers of the bill hoped that charter schools might provide options to boost public school education.

One of the Missouri charter school law's strengths is that it allows state public higher education institutions to sponsor charter schools. In a number of states, charter schools can only be sponsored by local school boards which often have no interest in ceding any control. The Missouri charter school law also has some weaknesses. The law does not provide a funding mechanism for charter school buildings. Additionally, it only allows charter public schools to be created within the boundaries of the Kansas City, MO and St. Louis school districts. At the time, these two districts were widely viewed as failing by every standard so this was more politically palatable than trying to get a law passed that covered the whole state.

Chapter 4

University Academy

Shortly after Missouri passed its charter school law, my parents Shirley and Barnett Helzberg, Tom Bloch and Lynne Brown teamed up and started working together to start a college-preparatory charter school. The four co-founders believe deeply that students living in the Kansas City Missouri School District deserve the opportunity to have an excellent college preparatory education. The founders' initial vision was to establish a school that emphasizes college preparation, career development, community service and leadership. The mission of the new school was to prepare students to succeed in an institution of higher education and to become leaders in society. The founders chose the name University Academy because it reflected their aspirations for the school.

The idea for the school was further developed and refined. The founders enlisted Dr. Pat Henley, an education professor at the University of Missouri-Kansas City ("UMKC"), to help write University Academy's charter school application.

Dr. Henley was so enthusiastic about University Academy that she ended up leaving her position as a professor at UMKC to be the Founding Principal of the school.

UMKC agreed to sponsor the school's initial 5-year charter. University Academy received its charter in 1999 making it one of the first schools in Missouri to receive a charter under Missouri's charter school law. However, the founders spent an entire year planning before the school actually opened.

The school opened its doors in 2000, operating in a facility leased from UMKC located at 5605 Troost Avenue. In addition to providing University Academy the initial space for the school to operate and agreeing to sponsor the charter, UMKC has supported University Academy in many ways including providing an additional layer of oversight and guidance for both the board and administration. In 2005, UMKC renewed University Academy's charter — this time for 10 years.

As a result of the support and generosity of University Academy's board of directors and the Kansas City community, construction on a new

172,000 square foot state-of-the art facility began in 2004. When the new facility opened in August 2005, enrollment expanded from 300 students in grades 6-12 to roughly 1,000 students in Kindergarten through grade 12. Located at 6801 Holmes Road in Kansas City, Missouri, the school's campus provides a wonderful home for University Academy to pursue its mission.

The mission of University Academy is to prepare students to succeed in an institution of higher education and to become leaders in society. The vision of University Academy is to be the best K-12 college-preparatory charter public school in the country with an emphasis on college preparation, career development, community service and leadership.

As a charter public school, University Academy admits students on the basis of a random lottery drawn from a pool of applicants. All applicants must reside within the boundaries of the Kansas City Missouri School District. Open spots are first filled by random lottery from a preference pool comprised of applicants (1) who reside in a geographical area near the school or (2) who are siblings of existing University Academy students or (3) who are children of employees who live in the

KCMSD. Remaining spots are filled by random lottery from the general applicant pool. Presently, over 95% of the student body is African-American and roughly 75% qualify for free or reduced lunch.

Despite the fact that all of University Academy's students live within the boundaries of the Kansas City Missouri school district, the results at University Academy are dramatically different than the traditional school district.

In August 2015, Newsweek Magazine published their "America's top high schools" issue and ranked University Academy the 199th best high school in the country in the "beating the odds" category. Additionally, for the fifth year in a row, University Academy's high school was recognized for excellence by U.S. News & World Report.

For the 2015-2016 academic year, University Academy received 100% on its Annual Performance Report from the State of Missouri which equates to Accredited with Distinction. The Kansas City Missouri School District received a score of 70% which is actually their best performance in three decades.

University Academy's High School ranked #1 out of 397 public high schools based on state of

Missouri test scores for the 2015-2016 academic year[17]. Additionally, in 2016, University Academy's High School was one of fifty-four schools in the country to be named a National Title I Distinguished School. This honor, given by the National Title I Association, recognizes exceptional student performance.

In 2017 University Academy's High School was nominated for National Blue Ribbon Schools recognition. This award, given by the U.S. Department of Education, is considered the highest honor an American K-12 school can receive. Less than ½ of 1% of schools in the nation are nominated for the award in any given year. Accolades like this one are a reflection of the incredible commitment of University Academy's students, families, teachers, staff, administration, and supporters.

Throughout its history, 100% of University Academy's seniors have been accepted to college. Being accepted into a 4-year college is actually a requirement for high school graduation at University Academy. While college acceptance is a necessary step it is not success. The real measure of success is college completion. The 53% college completion rate for University Academy alumni is more than 5x the national average for students from lowest quartile income families (9%).

In recent years University Academy has started to focus on increasing the quality of colleges and universities to which UA students are applying. Over 50% of the class of 2016 was accepted to top 150 colleges or universities as ranked by US News & World Report. In 2016 University Academy hit a big milestone. One of our seniors was accepted to an Ivy League school. This was our first, but I am confident there will be many more in the future.

In addition to a rigorous academic program, there are a number of special programs and opportunities at University Academy which help prepare students for college including a significant emphasis on summer study abroad. We have found a high correlation between participation in summer study abroad while in high school and college completion. Summer study abroad experiences help prepare University Academy students to succeed in college and beyond. Additionally, these programs help students earn more scholarships and get into more top colleges. Seniors from University Academy's Class of 2016 who participated in summer study abroad were awarded an average of $240,000 in college scholarships versus $90,000 for students that didn't. The college completion rate for UA alums who participated in study abroad is 68% which is more than 7x the college completion rate for students from lowest quartile income families (9%).

University Academy still has many opportunities to improve as it seeks to fully realize the school's vision. Over time, the objective is to completely close the college completion gap between University Academy (53%) and highest quartile income students (77%).

Chapter 5

My Tenure as Chairman

In late 2003 my wife and I learned that we were expecting twins. We were living in New York City at the time and this made us want to be closer to family. Our boys were born in July of 2004 and we moved back to Kansas City in August of 2004. I joined the University Academy board around that same time.

It was a busy time at the school. University Academy was in the process of completing its new 172,000 square foot building. The new building opened for the 2005-2006 school year and at that time added grades K-5 giving it a complete K-12 program. In anticipation of opening a lower school, the school hired Cheri Shannon to be the Lower School Principal.

Prior to Cheri being hired, the school's sole academic leader had been Dr. Pat Henley. She was a very hands-on leader who was comfortable wearing many hats which was very valuable in the early days of the school. However, once the school moved into its new facility in 2005 and was a much larger operation, it became apparent that the administrative structure that was in place didn't fit the scale of the school. Other than Dr. Henley and the Lower School Principal, there was not much of an administrative team in place.

During the 2005-2006 school year, the board thought about and discussed what administrative structure would best position the school for success. During that time the board recognized that under any structure it was very important to hire a High School Principal. We engaged a top education search firm named Carney Sandoe to help recruit a world class High School Principal. During the search process Dr. Henley decided that she was going to retire at the end of the 2006-2007 school year.

By this time, the board had come to the conclusion that the best structure was a Superintendent / Executive Director with 3 principals reporting to that person. Now we were looking for both a High School Principal and a Superintendent. Although some of the candidates for the High School Principal position were considered for the Superintendent position, the board promoted Cheri Shannon, the Lower School Principal, to be Superintendent. The High School

Principal search led to the hiring of Dr. Clem Ukaoma who is in that position today and has created a consistently high performing, mastery-based learning high school.

Over the course of the next couple years I learned a lot about how the school worked as well as what was happening at some of the best charter schools around the country. Although University Academy had a terrific facility and was significantly outperforming the traditional school district, our academic performance was good, but not great.

As a result of how much better we were doing than the traditional district, there was some level of satisfaction among the founding board members about University Academy's performance. As I looked at the results of some of the best charter schools around the country, I felt like we could do a lot better.

In July 2007, I was elected to be Chairman of the board. I like to say I took over in a bloodless coup. My father had been Chairman of the school before me and was happy to pass the baton seeing my passion for the school's mission and my sense of urgency around excellence.

In a conversation about how we were going to go from good results to excellent results, Dr. Joe Nathan, shared the idea of creating a set of annual goals to hold the school's administration accountable for progress. He recommended adopting SMART goals (specific, measureable, achievable, realistic, and time-bound). One of the first things I implemented once I became Chairman was adopting an annual set of school goals. We adopted our first set of goals in 2007-2008 and have adopted annual goals every year since then.

On several occasions, Joe Nathan encouraged me to go visit some of the most successful charter public schools in the country. In October, 2007, I went with a group from University Academy and visited KIPP and YES Prep schools in Houston to see what we could learn. At these schools, students from low-income families consistently demonstrate academic achievement at the highest levels. Visiting KIPP and YES Prep and seeing what was being accomplished dramatically increased my expectations about what we could achieve at University Academy. These schools were amazing and there was lots of overlap in their approaches. KIPP and YES Prep operate with extremely high expectations and standards. The schools' missions are clear and visible. Students wear uniforms, data is embraced, and more instructional time is provided. Accountability is embedded in the culture at these schools. Faculty, staff, and administrators believe strongly in the schools' mission.

In May of 2008, we engaged a consultant named John Deadwyler (Bernard Consulting) to help our board with strategic planning. We began our strategic planning retreat with a discussion of our mission and vision. It quickly became clear that our vision was not aspirational and did not describe what we were trying to accomplish. Instead of writing a strategic plan, we ended up spending a full day discussing our mission and vision with a majority of the day spent on the vision. We reaffirmed our mission and crafted a vision statement that codified the aspirations of the school. Here is the vision that came out of that day:

"Our vision is to be the best K-12 college-preparatory charter public school in the country with an emphasis on college preparation, career development, community service and leadership."

At the end of the 2007-2008 school year we implemented a Superintendent review process which incorporated an upward review as well as looking at how we did on our annual goals. We didn't achieve many of the goals that year. Early in the 2008-2009 school year Cheri told us she planned to leave at the end of the school year. We were once again in the search game, this time engaging another education search firm named Hazard, Young, and Attea to help us find a Superintendent that could help us achieve our vision.

We had clear thoughts about the type of leader we were looking for. It was someone who had a strong conviction that low-income students could achieve at the highest levels and had demonstrated that they could get results. We ended up hiring a Superintendent from a much larger traditional school district in another state. She seemed like the right person to take the school to the next level. She asked for a 3-year contract, which is pretty typical in the traditional public school world. Although we had never had a contract, we agreed to have one.

This Superintendent was at University Academy for only 2 ½ years. In January of 2012 she accepted an interim position with the Kansas City Missouri School district which was in a crisis because their Superintendent John Covington had accepted a job in Detroit.

Our departed Superintendent did not leave us with a leadership team, in fact she had eliminated both the lower school and middle school principals. The only logical person we could have made acting Superintendent was our high school principal, but we really needed him in that position. As a result, the board gave me administrative control of the school until we could find an interim Superintendent.

I started spending a lot more time at the school. In addition to leading regular weekly meetings with senior staff and approving expenditures, I focused on 3 things: putting in place Principals at the middle and lower schools, hiring an interim Superintendent, and working on submitting our accreditation documents.

Leslie McTighe, a lower school teacher, had been appointed to be the lower school Principal starting July 1, 2012. I asked Ms. McTighe to step up and start taking on Principal duties for the lower school effective immediately. Ashley Knapp, the Lower School instructional coordinator also helped provide administrative leadership at the lower school. Ms. Knapp was later promoted to Assistant Principal.

We created a middle school principal position description and advertised the opening. I had been very impressed with a former administrator named Rebecca Gudde and reached out to her to see if she might be willing to apply for the Middle School Principal position. We were extremely fortunate that she was willing to come back. Ms. Gudde has subsequently been promoted to Assistant Superintendent and has played a major role in University Academy's success.

Once I stepped in, I learned that we were supposed to submit a number of documents related to accreditation in one month. These were documents that are typically worked on for a year before submission. Unfortunately, we were starting from scratch. I worked closely with the team to write the documents over the next month and we were able to submit them on schedule. While it was not ideal to pull together the accreditation documents in one month, the process of working together on a short deadline brought the team together in a very positive way.

Although we moved quickly, the process to hire an interim Superintendent still took over two months. We ended up hiring Dr. Maggie Anderson as our interim Superintendent. She had retired after a successful tenure at Knob Knobster, a district outside of Kansas City where Whitman Air Force Base is located. She was extremely strong, balanced, and fair which was exactly what we needed. Her leadership was calming and reassuring to staff. She successfully led the school through the accreditation visit in her first couple of weeks on the job.

While all of this was happening, the board engaged a search firm to help us with the search for a new Superintendent. We hired a firm named Koya Partners which specializes in education reform school leaders. We started our process in February of 2012 which is arguably very late. While our consultant was able to pull together some candidates, the process did not end with the board making an offer to a candidate. Fortunately, Dr. Maggie Anderson, who had initially signed on for a 4-month interim position, agreed to stay on for the 2012-2013 school year so we could find the right permanent leader for the school.

In the Fall of 2012 we went through a second Superintendent search process with Koya. We ended with one finalist candidate, but the board was not unified that this person was the right person. We did not make an offer. At that point, we decided to part ways with Koya.

In January of 2013, we hired a Kansas City based search firm called EFL Associates for a third search process. EFL Associates does not specialize in K-12 education searches and thus had no existing stable of candidates and also was not precluded from recruiting certain candidates that they had previously placed.

EFL successfully helped us find an excellent Superintendent. Tony Kline started with us on May 1, 2013 and is a fantastic Superintendent. Tony has very high expectations, is data driven, and is a team builder. He approaches everything at the school in a business-like way. He has the management skills to lead a high performing school and our results during his tenure reflect his leadership. Under Tony's leadership the school has really hit its stride and is arguably now one of the best open admission college-preparatory public schools in the country.

Despite relatively high turnover at the Superintendent level since I have been Chairman, the school has managed to continuously increase its performance. I believe this was possible, to a great extent, because of the school's very clear mission and vision. Additionally, having a set of board adopted annual goals has been an incredibly valuable practice that has kept the board, administration, and faculty focused on making the school better each year.

Since 2004, I have seen firsthand the transformative power of education. Students from any background can achieve at very high levels, go on to complete college, and be successful in the workplace. The trajectory of students' lives can be completely transformed through access to a high-quality education.

Today we have alumni who are having great success in their careers. A number of them are now coming back to support the school as speakers, mentors, and as financial supporters. Seeing the success of our alumni is incredibly rewarding.

While I acknowledge that low-income students need more supports and special programs to achieve at the highest levels, they clearly have the potential because they are doing it at University Academy and hundreds of charter public schools around the country.

The author congratulating 2015 Valedictorian
Nosa Eke who attends the University of Missouri.

The author congratulating University Academy's Class of 2016 Valedictorian Jazmyne Smith who attends the University of Pennsylvania. Our first Ivy Leaguer, however I am confident we will have many more in the future.

Chapter 6

Role of the School Board

Like any organization, a successful school starts with its board. Having a board that acts in the best interests of its students and the community is critical. The board oversees the school and works to ensure that the management, programs, and policies of the school result in the achievement of the school's mission and progress towards its vision.

A high performing board must be comprised of a committed group of volunteers whose only agenda is to provide the highest quality education possible to its students. Board members should have no conflicts or pre-conceived agendas as it relates to the school. They must have very high expectations and be passionate about the mission and vision of the school. They must be committed to running the school for the benefit of the students which sometimes means making hard decisions that may not be popular with staff broadly or individual staff members.

One major advantage charter public schools have over traditional public schools is the way their boards are structured. Traditional public school boards are publicly elected which means that all of the members are likely to have somewhat different priorities. Charter public schools are typically governed by a self-perpetuating board. New board members can be selected deliberately based on what expertise and experience they can bring to the board. Also, by ensuring that new board members believe strongly in the school's mission and vision, the likelihood of having a unified board is increased dramatically. Finally, charter schools have a larger pool of potential board candidates; while many excellent board candidates are unlikely to run for an elected school board, they will enthusiastically serve on a charter public school board.

A board's responsibilities include: (1) Creating a clear mission and vision, (2) Creating a culture of high expectations and accountability, (3) selecting and evaluating the school's superintendent, (4) ensuring the school's offerings are aligned with the school's mission and vision, (5) setting and adopting annual goals for the school, (6) Making policies and strategic decisions for the school and, (7) providing fiduciary oversight including approving the school's annual budget.

Board Role 1 – Create a very clear mission and vision

It is the board's role to ensure that the school has a very clear mission and vision. Operating without a clear mission and vision is like driving a car without knowing where you are heading. Having a really clear mission and vision is critical for a high performing school.

At University Academy, our mission is to prepare students to succeed at an institution of higher education and to become leaders in society. Our vision is to be the best K-12 college-preparatory charter public school in the country with an emphasis on college preparation, career development, community service and leadership.

Having a strong vision has helped us significantly improve the school. Our mission and vision are our benchmarks to compare all of our activities against. Given that our mission is college prep and our vision is to be the best, the ultimate measure of our success is the percentage of our alums that complete a college degree. Every school should consider how they can measure their effectiveness versus their mission and start measuring it.

A school's mission and vision should be broadly displayed throughout the school for staff, students, parents, and all stakeholders to see. This helps create a community that is working together to accomplish the same thing. The learning environment should also reflect the school's mission. For example, we display college pendants for each institution our alumni attend on our Wall of Honor. Under each pendant are the names of alums who are attending or have graduated from that college or university. Also each teacher's name plate outside their classroom includes their alma mater.

In addition, to a mission and vision, it is helpful to have a set of core school values. For example, the learning environment at University Academy is fostered by four core values. These core values are:

- All students can achieve at the highest levels
- University Academy will promote students to the next grade only when they can demonstrate the required knowledge (no social promotion)
- All University Academy students are expected to attend and graduate from college
- More time on task benefits students (longer school day and school year)

Everything should flow from a school's mission, vision, and core values.

Board Role 2 – Create a culture of high expectations and accountability

Extremely high expectations are essential. These expectations relate to both what students can achieve and in regards to the quality of programs provided. This is especially important for schools serving low-income students. Board members must have a strong conviction that low-income students have the potential to achieve at the highest levels. Like all students, low-income students need a great education as well as services and opportunities. If the mission of the school is college-preparatory the board should also have an expectation that all students will attend and graduate from college. My own litmus test for what is good enough for the students at University Academy is my own children. If it is not good enough for my own children, then it is not good enough for the students at University Academy.

The board is responsible for creating a system of accountability that pervades the school's operations and culture. At University Academy we have developed a number of processes that promote accountability. For example:

- We do an annual formal evaluation of our Superintendent.
- All teachers and staff have a formal annual evaluation. Part of teacher's evaluations are based on the Network for Educator Effectiveness (NEE) evaluation tool.
- We adopt annual goals and create a scorecard at the end of each year to examine what was and wasn't accomplished.
- We perform internal assessments throughout the year and utilize the data to adjust teaching and curriculum.
- We have a time-bound strategic plan and look at what progress has been made on a monthly basis.

Board Role 3 – Hire a great Superintendent and perform an annual evaluation

One of the board's most important responsibilities is selecting and hiring the administrative leader of the school whether it is a Superintendent, Executive Director, or CEO. There are many folks who hold these titles, who unfortunately do not have the right skill set to be successful.

Since 2004, I have worked with 5 different school leaders and have learned a lot about what type of school leader is most effective as well as the process of hiring and evaluating Superintendents. The Superintendent sets the tone for the team and can either put the school on a path to continuous improvement or create a toxic environment.

The typical path for school leaders is that they start out as teachers and they do well. They then get promoted to a Principal position and if they do well at that they are considered for a Superintendent position. Unfortunately, great teachers are not necessarily great managers. Just because someone is a great Principal it does not mean they will be a great Superintendent.

In addition to being a talented educator, the right Superintendent must believe in and be passionate about the mission and vision of the school. He/she must be a good communicator. He/she must have enough of a financial background to understand a budget and allocate capital in the most efficient and effective way possible. He/she must know how to hire great people and build a team. He/she must be able to delegate. He/she must understand school operations including food service, busing, facilities, and risk management. Finally, they must be a person of the highest integrity and understand that both good and especially bad news needs to be shared with the Board.

Hiring a new Superintendent is arguably the board's hardest and most important responsibility. Having been involved in multiple searches with four different search firms, I have found search firms to be helpful for putting in place a good process and advertising the position. However, education search firms have a stable of candidates that they are putting in front of search committees. They are not necessarily the best candidates, yet the search firm gets paid when the board hires a candidate so the search committee needs to be skeptical and do its own homework. For finalist candidates, the search committee should do its own reference checking – both on and off of reference list. While it is impossible to guarantee success, the board doing its own due diligence on candidates will increase the chances for a successful hire.

One question that is likely during the process of hiring a Superintendent relates to a contract. Some candidates may require one, but in my experience they are not particularly healthy for either party. Often contracts are for 3 years, so then after two years on the job it brings up the awkward conversation....will the contract be renewed or extended? In my experience the board/superintendent relationship is healthier if there is no contract. Then the person is on the job unless they are not performing or they decide to leave which is functionally the same as if they had a contract. A contract does little to protect the interest of the students. For example, it will not prevent performance issues or stop a Superintendent from accepting another job. The only potentially beneficial clause is a no cause termination provision which spells out how much the school can pay to get rid of a Superintendent who is not delivering for students. Sometimes contracts may be a necessary evil, but it is better for everyone if they can be avoided.

Superintendents should be evaluated on an annual basis. There are a variety of ways to do this. At University Academy we have developed a 360 degree review process that works well for us. First, all of the Superintendent's direct reports are surveyed (upward reviews). We use an outside consulting firm to manage this process and summarize the results. This provides an extra layer of anonymity which hopefully allows those people to comment freely. The summary of the upward reviews is then shared with the board. We also complete a scorecard of the annual goals so that the board can look at which goals were met and which were not. With these two pieces of information, as well as interactions throughout the year, each board member is surveyed and asked four questions:

- What is the Superintendent doing well?
- What are areas for improvement for the Superintendent?
- What is the Superintendent not doing that they should be doing?
- Rate the Superintendent's performance on a 1-10 scale.

Once again, we engage an outside consulting firm to manage this survey process and summarize results. The summary document then informs an annual review conversation between the Chairman and Superintendent. Occasionally another board member will participate in that discussion. The summary document is a guide for the annual review, but is not given directly to the Superintendent.

Our Superintendent has a discretionary bonus opportunity of up to 10% of their salary. The actual amount of the bonus is calculated 50% based on meeting the annual goals and 50% based on the average performance rating by the board.

A healthy relationship between the Superintendent and Board is critical for a high performing school. Communication should be frequent and open. High performing boards understand that not everything works or goes according to plan all the time.

The author and Superintendent Tony Kline at the
KMBZ studio talking about University Academy
on Live with Rink and Laura.

Use this URL to hear the interview:

http://www.livewithrinkandlaura.com/full-shows/friends-of-university-academy/

Board Role 4 - Ensure the school's offerings and programs are aligned with the school's mission and vision

Although choosing a specific curriculum for a course and implementing the curriculum are not Board duties, the Board should ensure that the overall course offerings of a school are in alignment with the school's mission and vision.

For a college-preparatory school like University Academy, it is critical that the academic program is rigorous so students are prepared to succeed in college. At University Academy this is put into practice in various ways.

At the lower school in the last quarter of a given year, the next year's standards are previewed. For example, second graders are exposed to third grade curriculum during the last quarter of the school year and during summer school. Lower school students have to hit achievement metrics to advance to the next grade. The school does not engage in social promotion. Students must have the required skills and knowledge to advance to the next grade. Less than 5% of students are held back each year.

At the Middle School course content and assessments are aligned with college-preparatory standards. Standards based grading is used. The writing requirements are demanding in regards to length and depth of assignments.

High School is based on mastery exams. For students to get the credit they must demonstrate a certain proficiency or they repeat or remediate during summer until they can demonstrate mastery. This rigid but straightforward system works well with high school students.

At the high school students are required to take 4 years of Math, English, Science, Social Studies, and Foreign Language. At the high school, we offer Advanced Placement courses, as well as dual credit classes through partnerships with Rockhurst University, UMKC and Metropolitan Community College. Dual credit courses offer the rigor of a college class and provide both high school and college credit. Finally, we have special electives which help prepare our students for leadership including junior / senior seminars, an entrepreneurship program and accounting classes.

All juniors and seniors take junior / senior seminar. This class is about selecting the right college, creating a compelling application, preparing for ACT tests, navigating financial aid, and learning skills that provide a foundation for success at college.

All students must be accepted to a 4-year college to graduate from University Academy. As a result of this requirement, 100% of University Academy seniors have been accepted to college since its first graduating class in 2004.

It is also the Board's responsibility to provide oversight of a school's extra-curricular offerings to ensure that they reflect the school's mission. At University Academy, having programs like debate, science olympiad, academic decathlon, robotics, and coding align with our mission versus more traditional extra-curricular programs. We also offer a range of sports including basketball, volleyball, football, and track & field. We don't just look at these programs as fun, but as a way of teaching teamwork and resilience. Additionally, our athletic program has generated a significant amount of athletic scholarships benefitting our students.

It is also the board's responsibility to go beyond the academic program and make sure the whole child is being addressed. At University

Academy most of our students come from low-income families. Thus we provide a number of extra services to support our students. Since we moved into our new facility in 2005, we have had an onsite health clinic through a partnership with Children's Mercy Hospital. The clinic addresses preventative items like vaccines and provides care for children who are sick. The clinic has been so successful that in 2012 we replicated the model and opened an onsite dental clinic in partnership with the University of Missouri-Kansas City's Dental School.

Additionally, University Academy has three counselors on staff as well as a social worker. These professionals address items that allow students to stay focused on being students.

Finally, through a program started by the Junior League of Greater Kansas City in partnership with Harvesters, an amazing food bank, we provide food items each week to food insecure students at the school. On Fridays, students that have been identified as food insecure are given a bag of food to take home on the weekend to ensure that they come in Monday morning ready to learn.

Board Role 5 - Set and Adopt SMART Goals for each school year

Adopting a set of annual goals is a very simple management tool which, while extremely common in the business world, is very rare in the education world. This practice has been integral to the success we have achieved at University Academy.

Each year our board adopts a set of annual goals, typically there are 10-12 goals each year. A number of these carry over from year to year, however others are not repeated. Once the board has adopted annual school goals, they are prominently posted in key locations around the school for everyone to see. This helps keep students, faculty, and parents all focused on what the goals are. There is no mystery about what we are trying to accomplish.

The school goals cover a range of items including academic achievement on state tests, attendance, ACT scores, and college acceptance to selective schools. In my experience, once we have started measuring an item, we have achieved great results. A perfect example is admission to top 150 schools. For the 2013-2014 school year, our

Superintendent Tony Kline suggested we adopt a goal that 20% of our seniors would be accepted to top 150 schools based on US News & World Report Rankings. At the end of the year 35% of our seniors had been accepted by these schools. For 2014-2015, the goal was moved up to 40% and 49% of our seniors were accepted to top 150 schools. For 2015-2016 the goal was 50% and 53% of our seniors were accepted to top 150 schools. This illustrates the power of adopting written goals.

Some of our goals are based on standardized test results. Standardized testing is a controversial topic, but I am not sure why. The tests measure things like math skills, vocabulary, and reading comprehension. Those are things our students have to be good at if they are going to have the opportunity to go to a top college and pursue any career they desire. Being advanced / proficient on the tests is a by-product of learning. It is a minimum hurdle, not the ultimate objective which is beyond that and includes critical thinking, problem solving, written and verbal communication skills, research and organizational skills, and resilience. I highly encourage folks involved in traditional or charter schools to embrace testing and the data it provides.

At University Academy, under our current Superintendent, we have developed a robust internal assessment program. Tests are given on a schedule throughout the year. Data teams meet weekly to analyze the data gleaned from these internal assessments and teaching and curriculum are adjusted as necessary. This has been very beneficial. Incorporating the use of data is a very important practice for high performing schools.

Board Role 6 – Board makes strategic decisions and creates policies

The board is responsible for making strategic decisions and creating policies. It is the responsibility of administration to execute on strategic plans and implement board policy. The board must understand its role and stay out of administrative functions.

It is the board's role to approve strategic decisions for the school. This could range from adopting a new merit based compensation plan to approving a capital project to drafting and approving a new strategic plan.

At University Academy we have found that having a well thought out strategic plan with time-bound objectives has been tremendously valuable. A high-quality strategic plan encapsulates where the school wants to be over a period of time (e.g. 5 years) and works backwards outlining what needs to be accomplished and in what time period. A strategic plan should not be placed on a shelf, but instead should be used to guide administration. We look at our progress on the objectives outlined in our strategic plan on a monthly basis.

In regard to policy, most K-12 schools have a policy manual which includes a set of written policies that have been adopted by the board. Policies can be updated anytime by the board and occasionally policies need to be updated as laws or circumstances evolve.

School policies cover many topics including employment related matters, student affairs, and school operations. Here are some examples of issues boards may face and how we have handled those issues:

Student Affairs Policies

Should students be required to wear uniforms?

At University Academy students are required to wear a uniform which helps create an orderly and focused learning environment. It should be noted that uniforms are required at almost every high performing charter public school around the country.

Employment Policies

Should there be a no-nepotism employment policy?

At University Academy no relatives of current employees can be hired. This is in the best interest of students to ensure that the best candidate is hired for each position. Having relatives as candidates complicates the hiring and firing process.

Should employees be required to sign a binding arbitration agreement as a condition of employment?

In education, unfortunately employment related litigation is extremely common. I was once told that the traditional public school system in Kansas City, MO typically has roughly 200 open employment related legal matters at any given time. During the 2011-2012 school year, Mike Blumenthal, University Academy's attorney suggested we consider implementing a policy whereby signing a binding arbitration agreement would be a condition of employment at the school.

Arbitration is simply a quicker and less expensive procedural mechanism than litigation for resolving employment disputes. An arbitration agreement provides the arbitrator with the very same authority to provide the very same remedy as any judge or jury could provide – just in a procedural forum that permits a speedier, less expensive, and less disruptive resolution of the dispute. Generally, plaintiff's attorneys are much less interested in pursuing arbitration cases because non-meritorious claims are much less likely to be successful given that the case is decided by a professional arbitrator (typically an attorney).

Many well-known Missouri companies including Hallmark and Anheuser-Busch make binding arbitration a condition of employment. Since we adopted this policy in late February of 2012, we have not had any lawsuits. This policy was absolutely the right choice as it has allowed UA to focus its time and money on our students rather than spending time and money litigating employment complaints.

School Operations Policies

How long should the school day and year be?

The board approves the school calendar. This allows the board to ensure that the length of the school year and day is aligned with the mission of the school.

Board Role 7 – Plays a fiduciary role including adopting an annual budget

The board acts as a fiduciary for the school. In addition to engaging an independent auditor to audit the school on an annual basis, the board approves the school's budget and plays a general oversight role in relation to the school's financial affairs.

It is extremely important that timely and accurate financial information is available to the board. At University Academy, in the monthly board packet, University Academy's CFO, Ron Zigeler, provides a current balance sheet as well as an income statement. Like many schools,

University Academy uses cash accounting so a cash flow statement is not needed. In addition, Mr. Zigeler provides a number of charts that show how the revenues and expenses are trending versus prior years. This is extremely helpful because the school year is front-loaded with expenses related to the beginning of the academic year.

The CFO does not just do the accounting, but also works with the Superintendent and Finance Committee to look for ways the organization can be more efficient and strategic in its spending. Our Finance Committee spends a lot of time looking at big expenditure items including busing, food service, and utilities.

It is the Superintendent's job to make sure the school has the right people to produce accurate and timely financial reports. If the school does not have the right people or a full-time CFO is not in the budget, another option is to outsource the financial reporting and accounts payable work to an accounting firm.

While the budget is prepared by administration, the board plays an important oversight role and should understand expenses associated with all major items including salaries, facilities, food service, utilities, and busing. The budget is not just an accounting of money coming in and out, it reflects the strategic priorities of the school.

Each year, after the close of the fiscal year, the board should engage an independent auditor to verify the school's financial reporting. When the auditors present their report, the board or some portion of it should meet with the auditor without any administration present. We always ask about any areas of concern and what the auditor would do differently if he/she were the CFO.

Each month in the board materials a warrant list is included. The warrant list reflects all payments made by the school during the prior month. Board members are expected to look through the list and ask questions. Checks written by the school must be signed by two people…the Superintendent and all board members are signers.

The board should also understand the sources of funding for the school. In Missouri, schools receive funding based on average daily attendance – the total number of students multiplied by the attendance rate. Thus attendance is not only important for educational reasons, but also for the finances of the school. This is why each year one of the annual goals at University Academy is about the school's attendance rate.

The board at University Academy has a two-person Finance committee that meets with the school's CFO and Superintendent on a monthly basis. The finance committee members have strong financial backgrounds and dig deeper into financial matters with the CFO and Superintendent. The Finance committee may also recommend approval of certain items to the full board. At University Academy, the Finance Committee is also responsible for making decisions about the manner any surplus funds on the school's balance sheet are invested. At some schools this is handled by a separate investment committee.

Chapter 7

The People Who Make It Happen

The "not so" secret to University Academy's success, like all other high performing schools, is great teachers and staff. Operating a high performing public school is not rocket science. There is no secret sauce or magic bullet. However, talented and dedicated teachers and administrators are a requirement. The biggest difference between terrific and mediocre schools is very strong leadership.

I have heard some educators explain that poverty is the cause of low academic achievement in America's urban school districts. However, hundreds of high performing charter public schools around the country have demonstrated the fallacy of this explanation by consistently demonstrating that low-income students can achieve at the highest levels. While poverty and low academic achievement are highly correlated, poverty does not cause low academic achievement. Poorly run school districts, schools, and classrooms are the cause of low academic achievement. Unfortunately, weak districts, schools, and teachers tend to be concentrated in low-income areas.

The difference between having an excellent teacher and a poor one is huge for students. Thomas Kane, a Harvard researcher, found that students "who are taught by a teacher in the bottom 5% of competence lose 9.54 months of learning in a single year compared to students with average teachers."

Having a teaching certificate does not make an individual an effective teacher. At University Academy, we have deliberately put in place policies and practices to recruit and retain highly effective teachers and staff. We take the hiring process very seriously and put a lot of energy into interviewing and screening applicants.

When we have an opening, we broadly advertise the opportunity and have a specific deadline for applications. We encourage excellent candidates to apply. The interview process is multi-faceted and is not just about credentials and experience. We want to make sure the candidate is passionate about teaching, strongly believes that all students can achieve at the highest levels and that they embrace our college preparatory mission.

We did an internal study on our faculty at University Academy and found that there was a positive correlation between ACT / SAT scores and effectiveness in the classroom. As a result of this finding, we implemented a minimum 21 ACT/SAT equivalent score cut-off which has made our hiring process more efficient and effective. This single requirement eliminates about 70% of the candidates.

Experience at a high-performing school matters. We have had a lot of success hiring teachers and administrators from excellent rural and suburban traditional school districts. We have found that candidates who have taught at or been administrators at high performing schools understand what is required for high academic achievement. This experience and the wisdom gained from it usually translates to success at our school.

Our compensation philosophy is different than most traditional public schools. The typical way of paying teachers is based on a simple scale that takes into account academic credentials and years of experience. This type of system results in some average teachers getting paid much more than some excellent teachers. This makes little sense given that effective instruction is arguably the single most important factor for high academic achievement.

We have always believed in pay for performance. We believe teachers can be effectively evaluated. There is little controversy about teachers evaluating students. Why is evaluating teachers such a controversial topic? There are a number of ways to evaluate teachers. At University Academy, we currently use an evaluation tool from the Network for Educator Effectiveness (NEE). Teachers' evaluations are based:

40% on NEE observations
5% on unit of instruction
15% on professional development plan
20% on student achievement
10% on parent relations
5% on professionalism
5% on teamwork

Over the years, we have tried various compensation systems to reward outstanding teachers for their performance. Under our current system, teachers that are high performers receive higher salary increases than teachers that are not high performers. Excellent teachers should be rewarded for their performance. Teachers must be observed regularly, given professional development, and reviewed at least annually. If teachers are not effective in the classroom, they should not be in front of students.

One of the largest problems in K-12 education is that there is very little individual accountability. Most traditional public schools offer tenure to teachers after a period (sometimes as short as two years) with little or no consideration of the teacher's effectiveness in the classroom. This is due to collective bargaining agreements that are supposed to protect teachers, but have actually damaged our country by taking accountability out the K-12 education system.

All children can achieve at very high levels if they are in a well-managed school with great teachers and administrators. The importance of great teachers and administrators cannot be overstated. High performing schools recognize the importance of great faculty and staff and are intentional in the way they recruit and manage their team members.

Chapter 8

Friends of University Academy

Mary Bloch is married to Tom Bloch, a co-founder of the school, and has been very involved in helping the school succeed since its inception. In the first couple years of University Academy's existence, Mary recognized the need and importance for University Academy to get support from the community. Mary created and chaired the school's inaugural fundraiser in 2003. Mary chaired or co-chaired the event in 2004 and 2005 as well. Mary laid the foundation for the amazing community support University Academy has received since its inception.

From 2003 through 2009 the event was handled by volunteers and a staff member at the school. This arrangement was always a little awkward in that we wanted the school focused on education, yet a staff member was focused on fundraising and naturally this took some focus away from education. Gala funds were used to support a number of special opportunities for students including college trips, summer study abroad scholarships, ACT test prep courses, and partnerships with organizations like Kansas City Young Audiences.

In 2004 University Academy had its first graduating class. My father, who was Chairman of the Board at the time, believed that we needed to stay in touch with our graduates. This idea was inspired by a visit to Wallin Education Partners in Minneapolis. This organization is focused on helping low-income students attend and graduate from college. Early on, Wallin realized that financial aid alone was not enough so they developed a comprehensive array of persistence services to increase the impact of their scholarship program.

Initially the responsibility for tracking our alumni fell on the high school college counselor. At some point, in addition to tracking, we started sending care packages to our alumni at college. After 5 years of tracking our alumni and seeing that a significant number of them were not staying in college, we recognized the need for a more comprehensive alumni support program. The complexity was that we couldn't spend K-12 dollars on an initiative for alumni.

For lots of reasons it made sense to start a separate nonprofit entity to support the mission of the school. In 2010, I incorporated Friends of University Academy, a 501(c)3 not-for-profit. Friends of University Academy's founding board members were Mary Bloch, Vicki Reisler, and myself.

Friends of University Academy ("Friends of UA") provides funding for and facilitates a number of special programs and opportunities for K-12 students. Additionally, Friends of UA operates a program which supports alumni of University Academy in their pursuit of their academic and career goals. I cover the details of this program in the next chapter.

Programs for K-12 students include partnerships with external organizations like Kansas City Young Audiences, as well as experiences like college trips. Additionally, Friends of UA facilitates and provides scholarships for middle school students to attend sleep away summer camps. At the Upper School, Friends of UA puts a significant emphasis on sending students on summer study abroad programs with the Experiment in International Living and Students Diplomacy Corps. Friends of UA also provides scholarships for summer wilderness leadership courses with the National Outdoor Leadership School (NOLS).

In addition to exposing students to international issues, study abroad helps students build confidence and develop life skills and resilience. These skills help UA alums succeed in college and beyond. Additionally, these experiential learning opportunities help students earn more scholarships, get into top colleges, and complete college.

- Seniors from University Academy's Class of 2016 who participated in summer study abroad were offered an average of $240,000 in college scholarships versus $90,000 for students that did not.
- 76% of the 2016 seniors who participated in study abroad were accepted to top 150 colleges versus 30% of the students that did not.
- The college completion rate for UA alums who participated in study abroad (while in high school) is 68% which is more than 7x the college completion rate for students from lowest quartile income families (9%).

Given these amazing statistics, we believe summer study abroad scholarships are an extremely high return philanthropic investment. As a result of this, we have put a lot of effort into growing our summer study abroad program. 71% of University Academy's Class of 2017 will have participated in summer study abroad while in high school. This is likely one of the highest study abroad participation rates for a public high school in America.

In addition to providing special educational programs and opportunities for K-12 students at UA and operating the Alumni Success Program, Friends of UA engages the community to raise funds for its programs and also create awareness about University Academy, the importance of education, and the value of charter schools. Since its founding in 2010, staff at Friends of UA have taken the lead on working with the volunteer chair or chairs to make the annual gala fundraiser happen.

Friends of UA also puts on special events to engage the community. For example, it hosted a screening of the movie Waiting for Superman and more recently hosted a screening of An American Ascent. It brought Wes Moore to Kansas City for a community event and to speak at graduation. Friends of UA also organizes lunches a couple of times a year at the school and invites community members to learn about what is happening at the school.

Friends of University Academy started out with 1 staff member. Lesley Creal facilitated our annual gala and also tracked our alums and sent care packages. Lesley also provided a number of services to our alumni including counseling and internship support. As our alumni base grew it became apparent that we needed more resources dedicated to our Alumni Support Program. In 2011 we hired David Rucker, a Teach for America alum, to be the Director of the Alumni Success Program.

David helped define the Alumni Success Program and added a number of programs as well. One major addition to the Alumni Support Program was the College Incentive Program (CIP) which helps our alumni with out-of-pocket college expenses.

The costs of attending college are very high and financial aid and student loans do not cover all expenses. Students from low-income families (earning less than $36,100) face an average annual out-of-pocket cost (after grants, scholarships, loans, and other aid) of $10,400 to attend a 4-year public college full-time. This represents at least 28% of a low-income family's yearly pre-tax income. In comparison, students from high-income families ($104,600 or more) pay on average $18,400 in out-of-pocket expenses which represents at most 17.6% of their family's annual pre-tax income to attend a 4-year public institution full-time[18].

As the above data demonstrates, it is extremely challenging for low-income families to provide meaningful financial support to a family member who is pursuing a college degree. Financial strain and lack of money are commonly cited reasons for why students drop out of college. According to With Their Whole Lives Ahead of Them (a report by Public Agenda funded by the Bill and Melinda Gates Foundation), 85% of students that dropped out of college before graduation identified financial reasons for leaving. More specifically, 54% cited the need to work to earn money and 31% cited the difficulty of paying college tuition and fees.

The purpose of the College Incentive Program is to increase college completion rates by providing unrestricted financial support to University Academy alumni who are in college and are meeting certain grade point average benchmarks

($500 per semester for a prior semester GPA of 2.5, $750 for a GPA of 3.0, and $1000 for a GPA of 3.5). All UA alums are eligible up to 8 semesters. The program provides money to cover things not typically included in scholarships like food, books, transportation, clothes, and a computer.

In 2014 Lesley decided to leave us to spend time with her young children. Before she left I asked her to find her replacement which was no easy task given what a great job she had done. Lesley and David interviewed a number of great candidates and they ended up recommending Maria Dickson to be the Director of Community Engagement. Maria became responsible for our fundraising as well as planning and executing community events including our annual gala.

Subsequently we added another team member Kristin Moats, a returned Peace Corps Volunteer who served in Swaziland. Kristin helps direct our Alumni Success Program including the CIP program. Additionally, she manages our summer scholarships for middle school sleep-away camp and study abroad and NOLS at the high school.

In 2015 David Rucker was promoted to be the first ever Executive Director of Friends of University Academy. The organization operates out of my office in Kansas City and has a $1 million budget for the 2016-2017 fiscal year.

Since their inceptions, University Academy and Friends of University Academy have received an incredible amount of generous support from people in the community. These people have been integral to the school's success. The programs operated and funded by Friends of University Academy have helped make University Academy a high performing school.

Friends of University Academy's 2016 Passport to Success gala highlighted the impact of summer study abroad opportunities with the Experiment in International Living and Student Diplomacy Corps. Funds from the gala help pay for scholarships for University Academy high school students to participate in these programs. Over 71% of University Academy's class of 2017 will have participated in summer study abroad while in high school thanks to the generosity of our supporters.

Use this URL to see the gala video about the summer study abroad program:

https://vimeo.com/163263048

The 2015 Friends of University Academy "College Graduation" Gala highlighted Friends of UA's Alumni Success Program. This program supports UA alums as they pursue their academic and career goals after high school graduation. My wife Jamie and I chaired the event.

Use this URL to see the gala video about the Alumni Success Program:

https://www.youtube.com/watch?v=EFQmp1_mfuo

Chapter 9

Alumni Success Program

In the prior chapter I mentioned Friends of University Academy's Alumni Success Program (ASP). We believe this program is incredibly valuable and is an important compliment to the rigorous academic program and experiential learning opportunities at University Academy. I am only aware of a handful of K-12 organizations that actively support their alumni after high school graduation including KIPP through College, YES Prep's Alumni Support Program, and The SEED Foundation's College Transition & Success Program. I am not aware of any other alumni support programs that include financial awards for staying in college and meeting certain GPA milestones.

The Alumni Success Program takes over after high school graduation to help University Academy alumni achieve their academic and career goals. The ASP aims to increase the probability of success in an institution of higher education and level the playing field for University Academy alums by providing support, information and connections.

Here are the key Alumni Success Program Components:

Interaction with University Academy

- Juniors and Seniors in the high school have regular interaction with the ASP staff prior to graduation during junior/senior seminar classes and college trips
- Alumni are invited into the school to share their college and career experiences and for school events and reunions
- The ASP staff interacts with students, staff, and parents at all levels of the school to emphasize the goal of college graduation and the support available to that end

Alumni Tracking

- Current contact info for all alumni
- Status (in school, job status, etc.)

Coaching/Counseling

- Dedicated staff member available for alumni guidance and mentoring
- Direct alums to resources at their school

- Funding for outside resources for students if not available on their campus, such as tutoring, counseling, and study materials

Continued Life/Social Skills Education

- Provide alumni with information on a variety of topics including time management, budgeting, study habits, etc.

College Incentive Program (CIP)

- The CIP helps students pay for a variety of college expenses not covered by traditional scholarships including books, food, rent, and computers.
- The CIP rewards academic achievements reflected by prior semester grades.
  - $1000 for prior semester GPA of 3.5 or above
  - $750 for prior semester GPA of 3.0-3.49
  - $500 for prior semester GPA of 2.5-2.99
  - $500 for enrollment verification for first semester of college
- Requires full-time enrollment (minimum 12 credit hours) at a 2-year or 4-year college for prior and current semesters

- Eligibility lasts for 6 years after high school graduation
  - Maximum 8 semesters of undergraduate study
  - Up to 4 of the 8 semesters can be at a 2-year college
- Awards are based on the previous semester grades or first-semester undergraduate enrollment verification of full-time study
- Requires a copy of an official transcript including name, previous semester grades, and class list for the upcoming semester (Exceptions would be for 1st semester and graduating students)
- Requires a current address, phone number, and email; Also major or degree (if not on transcript)
- Friends of UA must have a signed Family Educational Rights and Privacy Act (FERPA) waiver on file

Mentoring

- Connect successful alums with alums in their freshman year of college
- Guidance on utilizing resources, networking, making career decisions, and maintaining focus when faced with challenges

Community Building

- Regular communication with Alumni through email blasts and social media
- Semester care packages for students in college including notes from UA seniors
- Organized campus visits to meet with groups of Alumni at their college
- Individual and small group meetings over coffee or lunch with ASP staff
- Annual holiday party

Graduate School Counseling

- Counsel alumni on how to position themselves for graduate school where applicable (coursework, internships, application process, financing, etc.)
- Provide financial assistance for graduate school test prep courses such as - LSAT, GRE, GMAT

Career Acceleration

- Create partnerships with businesses and organizations willing to interview or offer UA Alums summer internships
- Facilitate the interview process

- Review and revise resumes, conduct mock interviews, facilitate networking
- Provide funding ($4,000 each) for eight-week summer internships with nonprofit organizations.

Networking/Job Search Support

- Work with alumni who have graduated or are graduating from college to facilitate interview opportunities in the industry of their choice
- Review and revise resumes, conduct mock interviews, facilitate networking
- Networking in the Kansas City area in various industries to provide alumni with opportunities for interviews and potential professional mentors
- Career coaching sessions provided for small groups of Alumni to learn from seasoned professionals and receive feedback about career goals and materials

Career Coaching
- Work with Alumni to develop strategic plans and create action items toward career goals
- Act as a sounding board to help Alumni navigate significant workplace challenges, decisions, and relationships

Chapter 10

How Charter Schools Have Changed the KCMSD

Many charter public schools have been started in Kansas City, MO since 1998. In Kansas City, there are now over 20 charter public schools serving over 10,000 students which represents roughly 40% of the students attending public schools within the boundaries of the KCMSD. Charter public schools' market share in Kansas City is in the top five in the nation behind only New Orleans, Detroit, and Washington, DC. It is roughly tied with Flint, MI.

Ten of Kansas City's charter schools opened their doors in 1999 which was the first year possible. Since then, more than a dozen new charter public schools have opened. KIPP, a national charter management organization, established a school in Kansas City in 2007. In 2011, the Kauffman Foundation established the Ewing Marion Kauffman School. Today there are a number of excellent schools in addition to University Academy including Academie Lafeyette (a K-8 French immersion school), Crossroads Academy, and the Ewing Marion Kauffman School.

In the fall of 2016 two new charter schools opened including one managed by the Citizens of the World charter school network. Additionally, the KCMSD sponsored its first charter school, the Kansas City Neighborhood Academy.

	Kansas City Charter Public Schools				
	Charter Public School	Charter Sponsor	Year Opened	2016 APR Score	Students
1	Academie Lafayette	UCM	1999-2000	97.5%	871
2	Academy for Integrated Arts	UMKC	2012-2013	66.0%	88
3	Allen Village Charter School	UMKC	1999-2000	95.6%	639
4	Alta Vista Charter School	UCM	1999-2000	73.2%	735
5	Benjamin Banneker Charter Academy of Technology	UCM	1999-2000	46.9%	334
6	Brookside Charter School	UMKC	2002-2003	70.6%	543
7	Citizens of the World	MCPSC	2016-2017	New	
8	Crossroads Academy	UCM	2012-2013	98.6%	280
9	DeLaSalle Charter School	UMKC	2010-2011	53.2%	299
10	Della Lamb Elementary	UCM	1999-2000	36.9%	602
11	Ewing Marion Kauffman School	MU	2011-2012	100.0%	532
12	Frontier School of Excellence	UMKC	2009-2010	84.3%	1,268
13	Genesis School	UMKC	1999-2000	43.1%	269
14	Gordon Parks Elementary	UCM	1999-2000	75.0%	126
15	Hogan Preparatory Academy Elementary School	UCM	1999-2000	68.4%	1,032
16	Hope Leadership Academy	UCM	2011-2012	75.0%	138
17	Kansas City Neighborhood Academy	KCPS	2016-2017	New	
18	KIPP Endeavor Academy	MU	2007-2008	70.6%	275
19	Lee A. Tolbert Community Academy	UMKC	1999-2000	66.3%	514
20	Pathway Academy	UMKC	2009-2010	55.6%	436
21	Scuola Vita Nouva	UCM	1999-2000	85.0%	200
22	University Academy	UMKC	2000-2001	100.0%	1,001
					10,182
	Kansas City Public Schools (Traditional Public School District)			70%	

Although a number of the charter schools in Kansas City are excellent, some charter schools perform the same or worse than the traditional district. Just because a school is organized as a charter school, success is far from guaranteed. As the above chart shows, 8 out of 22 KC charter schools received Annual Yearly Performance scores from the State of Missouri that were lower than the traditional KC school district.

The good news is that 14 out of 22 KC charter schools received a score that was higher than the traditional district. Additionally, there are mechanisms for non-performing charter schools to go away. Charters are granted by charter authorizers for a period of time (often 5 years). After some period of time, if a school is not producing results that are better than the traditional school district they should not be re-authorized and should cease to exist.

Since 1999 a number of charter public schools have been closed because they were not succeeding including Academy of Kansas City, Derrick Thomas Academy, Don Bosco Education Center, Hope Academy, Kansas City Career Academy, Renaissance Academy, Southwest Charter School, Urban Community Leadership Academy, and Westport Edison.

Once a school district has a critical mass of charter schools, market forces will also help ensure the quality of schools. All parents, including low-income parents, want the best for their children. Given the option, they will place their children in the best school available. An education system that offers choices, allows parents and students to find the best option. Students are no longer tied to a single failing school district or one educational approach. Students will enroll in the best available options and the schools that aren't producing results will naturally wither and disappear.

We are seeing this process happen now in Kansas City. New schools continue to enter the market and weaker schools are disappearing. The environment is getting more competitive. It is important to keep in mind that progress has not happened overnight. It has taken 15 years to get to the inflection point where we are today.

Excellent charter public schools operating alongside a traditional public school district create a competitive education landscape. Parents and students no longer have only one option. Charter public schools create an array of choices and schools are forced to compete based on quality to attract students. The community and the students are the beneficiaries.

Before charter public schools, there were no other free public school options so many parents were stuck with the traditional school district even if it was failing them. And the traditional district had no incentive to improve because it was a monopoly. Competition creates an incentive for all public schools, charter and traditional, to get better.

Historically, strong public school systems in America have been a key contributor to economic class mobility as well as democratic enlightenment. Unfortunately, in many of America's cities, strong public school systems have not existed for decades which is why charter public schools are critical and can play an important role in making more high-quality education available. Charter public schools are part of the public school system and a bunch of great ones can contribute to a strong public school system.

For the first time in decades there is optimism among some education reform practitioners that a majority of the seats in Kansas City, Missouri will be high-quality within the next 10 years. For this to happen, high-quality new schools need to continue to open, good schools need to be supported so that they can make the leap to being excellent, and low performing schools need to be closed.

Chapter 11

Response to Charter School Critics

Despite the incredible potential of charter public schools to help transform our failing urban school districts and the undeniable success of thousands of charter public schools, there are still critics who do not get it or don't want to get it. Much of what is in this chapter came from a piece written by Whitney Tilson. Whitney is a hedge fund manager and education reform zealot. He has been deeply involved in Teach for America and KIPP. I highly encourage anyone interested in education reform to get on Whitney's email list by sending a request to leilajt2+edreform@gmail.com.

Opponents of charter schools say that charter schools, get results by enrolling better than average students. This is not accurate. Students at charter public schools are chosen by random lottery. Admission is not selective and the demographics of most charter schools reflect the districts they serve. State laws that authorize charter schools were specifically designed to ensure that access is equal for all students living in a geographic area.

Opponents say that charter public schools harm traditional school districts. I would argue that the opposite is true. Competition from charter schools provides an impetus for traditional districts to improve. In Kansas City, the district has been going downhill for five decades. Only recently, with charter schools having 40% market share, have their results stabilized and started to improve. In fact, for the 2015-2016 school year, the Kansas City Missouri school district received a 70% (Annual Performance Score) APR score from the state of Missouri, its highest score in three decades. There are no examples of monopolies providing excellent service and the same is true in K-12 public education.

Another criticism of charter schools is that they place too much emphasis on tested subjects like reading and math. First of all, I would argue that there should be a lot of emphasis on these two subjects. If one is an excellent reader and is good at math, you can learn just about anything else. Without a strong foundation in these two areas, it is hard to learn other subjects. In some ways many traditional public schools face an either or choice because they are restricted by teachers' union collective bargaining agreements which prevent more instructional time. However, the vast majority of high performing charter schools, because they are able to extend their school day and year, not only place more emphasis on reading and math, but also offer more science, history, and arts than traditional public schools

Another criticism of charter schools is that they are privatizing education or that they are for-profit. While there are some for-profit charter school operators, they account for a minority of schools. As far as I am aware, the for-profit operators do not have a track record of creating high performing schools. I personally believe every dollar available should be spent on educating children so I am not a fan of the for-profit operators, however at the end of the day it boils down to results. For-profit or nonprofit, if a school isn't producing better results than the traditional district over some period of time (5 years), they should cease to exist. Nonetheless, all charter schools are public schools. They are accountable for all of the same things as traditional public schools including board meetings that are open to the public and financial transparency.

The fact that private citizens are involved in starting and managing high performing charter schools around the country is a great thing. The traditional public school systems have not been effective at engaging people who could have helped them. Frankly, urban traditional public school systems have failed students for so long that it is not surprising that community members who have a desire to help, didn't have the confidence that their money or time would be well spent working through dysfunctional traditional urban school districts. The talent and resources of many private citizens involved in charter schools has been a tremendous benefit to millions of students.

Charter schools, many of which were started by non-educators, have demonstrated that much better results are possible with the same funding and students. This is obviously very disruptive to the status quo so it is no surprise that there are vocal critics. Their criticisms are not supported by the facts and they do not offer any alternative paths to improving education. Access to high-quality education is too important to allow anyone to stand in the way of progress.

Chapter 12

Conclusion

Income inequality, civil rights, crime, and unemployment are critical issues facing our country today. Providing access to a high-quality K-12 education is at the core of progress on all of these issues.

The status quo of K-12 education in America's inner cities is completely unacceptable. All students deserve access to an excellent free public education that provides the foundation for success in today's economy. Fixing our nation's failing urban school districts should be a civil rights priority of the highest level.

There is no secret sauce to running a high performing school with students from low-income families. There are many approaches, but they all involve high expectations and standards, excellent teachers and administrators, accountability, and always putting students' interests first. Hundreds of charter public schools around the country have proven that low-income students can achieve at the highest levels.

My hope is that this book has demonstrated how charter public schools can help transform a community's educational opportunities. It is important to recognize that creating a competitive educational environment does not happen overnight and it is not a linear process. It has taken Kansas City more than 15 years to get to the inflection point where it is today. I believe that the competitive landscape in Kansas City will continue to develop and that many more high-quality education seats will be available within the next ten years.

I hope that this book will inspire others to play a role in improving education in their communities by:

- Being a school choice / charter school advocate
- Helping start a charter school if more high-quality schools are needed in their community
- Serving as a school board member
- Supporting high-quality schools, whether traditional or charter

ACKNOWLEDGMENTS

I would like to thank my wonderful wife Jamie for not only being a fabulous mother and wife, but for enthusiastically supporting me and believing in the importance of addressing the massive educational inequalities that exist within our country.

I would like to thank Tom Bloch, Lynne Brown, Barnett Helzberg, and Shirley Helzberg for founding University Academy. They believe deeply that all students deserve access to a high-quality college preparatory education and had the will and determination to say no to the status quo of the failing Kansas City, MO traditional public school district. They created a charter public school that has provided a high-quality education to a large number of students that would otherwise not have had it. They created a school where students from low-income families are achieving at the highest levels. This book is about how their vision became a reality.

I would like to acknowledge Dr. Joe Nathan from the Center for School Change whose passionate advocacy of charter schools put the founders of University Academy on the path to opening a charter public school. Joe has also been a great source of advice about how to make University Academy excellent throughout the school's history. Without Joe's wisdom and national perspective, we would not be where we are today.

I would like to acknowledge the people who have invested their precious time in University Academy by serving on the board throughout its history including the four founders, Robert Stevenson, Jamie Helzberg, Debbie Sosland-Edelman, Dr. Steve Green, Reverend Stan Archie, Damon Porter, Josh Rowland, Father Thomas Curran, Jonathan Angrist, Dr. Gersham Nelson, Dr. Bernard Franklin, Christine Kemper, David Dickey, and Nicole Jacobs-Silvey. The school has benefitted immensely from these people's wisdom.

I would like to acknowledge the contributions of Friends of University Academy board members including founding board members Mary Bloch and Vicki Reisler, as well as current board members Mindy Wilson, Byron White, Kit Smith, and Sonya Nutter. These people have helped guide an organization that is doing some of the most innovative and impactful education work in the country.

I would like to acknowledge the incredibly talented and dedicated faculty and staff at University Academy and Friends of University Academy. They make a tremendous impact on the lives of the 1000 students who walk through University Academy's doors each day, as well as our 450 alumni. They help show what is possible and the impact of their amazing work is felt far beyond the walls of University Academy.

I would like to thank people who read drafts of this book and offered comments including Jamie Helzberg, Daniel Shaw, Barnett Helzberg, Bob Litan, Richard Whitmire, David Rucker, Mindy Wilson, Micah Hyman, Heidi Zuckerman, Tony Kline, Corey Scholes, Soledad Hurst, and Dr. Joe Nathan. Of course, all content in the book and any errors are my responsibility alone.

I would like to acknowledge numerous other people who have been deeply involved in improving education in Kansas City including Corey Scholes, Aaron North, Munro Richardson, Alicia Herald, and Hannah Loftus. These people and others' dedication to making radical improvement in K-12 education has inspired me. All five of these people are connected with the Ewing Marion Kauffman Foundation.

The Kauffman Foundation, under the leadership of Carl Schramm from 2002 to 2012, made improving education in Kansas City, MO a major priority. In addition to supporting charter public schools in numerous ways, the Kauffman Foundation promotes the overall health of the K-12 ecosystem in Kansas City through its support of education related programs including Teach for America, Kansas City Teacher Residency, Leading Educators, and City Year. In 2011, Kauffman founded the Ewing Marion Kauffman School, a charter public school in Kansas City, MO.

Finally, I would like to thank the many friends who have encouraged me along the way through their words and support of University Academy and Friends of University Academy.

Notes

[1] See Melissa Korn's article, "Big Gap in College Graduation Rates for Rich and Poor, Study Finds" in the Wall Street Journal. February 3, 2015.

[2] U.S. Census Bureau, 2012, Table PINC-03; Internal Revenue Service, 2010.

[3] From the National Alliance for Public Charter Schools' website.

4

https://www.schooldigger.com/go/MO/schoolrank. aspx?level=3 (schooldigger.com).

[5] From Cato Institute Policy Analysis No. 298 by Paul Ciotti.

[6] From Cato Institute Policy Analysis No. 298 by Paul Ciotti.

[7] From Cato Institute Policy Analysis No. 298 by Paul Ciotti.

[8] From Cato Institute Policy Analysis No. 298 by Paul Ciotti.

[9] From Cato Institute Policy Analysis No. 298 by Paul Ciotti.

[10] From Cato Institute Policy Analysis No. 298 by Paul Ciotti.

[11] From Cato Institute Policy Analysis No. 298 by Paul Ciotti.

[12] From Cato Institute Policy Analysis No. 298 by Paul Ciotti.

[13] From Cato Institute Policy Analysis No. 298 by Paul Ciotti.

[14] From Cato Institute Policy Analysis No. 298 by Paul Ciotti.

[15] Alternative Public School Systems. Dr. Kenneth Clark. Harvard Educational Review. Volume 38 No. 1 Winter 1968.

[16] Interview with Franc Flotron. April 27, 2016.

[17]

https://www.schooldigger.com/go/MO/schoolrank. aspx?level=3 (schooldigger.com).

[18] Stats In Brief: What Is the Price of College? U.S. Department of Education. December, 2010.